Command Your Destiny

Prophetic Declarations with Divine Authority To Claim Your Prosperity, Healing, Breaking Barriers, Financial Freedom, Promotion, Family Success, All Round Breakthrough, ETC.

Command Your Destiny

By

Millstorm Caulomar

Copyright

No part of this publication may be reproduced or transmitted in any form or by any means, electronic or mechanical, including photocopy, recording or any information storage and material systems, without

permission in writing from the publisher.

OTHER BOOKS BY THE SAME AUTHOR BOTH WITH PEN NAME AND REAL NAME:

https://author.amazon.com/books

https://author.amazon.com/books

https://www.amazon.com/dp/B07PFX9K6B

Command Your Destiny

Table Of Content

Introduction 9

Chapter One: Immediate Called......................12

Appropriate allocation: 16

    Awareness for calling 20

    Peter's Call 22

    The Greater or Higher Call 27

    And what's the glory of the Lord?................32

    SUMMARY..41

    Prayer Points For My Family 43

Chapter Two: Designing and Building: 49

    Let's see how Moses was commission........51

    Moses..51

    Joshua 58

    Isaiah 67

    Jeremiah...71

    The Great Commission.................................77

Chapter Three: Trust in the Lord......................85

- Walk By Faith, Not By Sight 105

Chapter Four Prosperity Is the Will Of God ... 114

- What Is The Will Of God? 118
- What Is True Prosperity? 124
- The Rich Young Ruler 128
- God's Presence 134
- Divine Favor 136
- The Unity of God (Shalom) 137
- Divine Health 138
- The joy of the Lord 139
- God's Security {Divine Protection} 141
- Salvation is the Pillar of True Prosperity 144
- Prayer Points 154

Chapter Five: Good Health And Happiness ... 157

- Making The Right Choice 158
- The Great Picture 167
- Choice And Destiny 173
- Abraham 174
- Esau And Jacob 175
- Joseph 176
- Abimelech 177

Herod The Great 181
The Rod Of Moses 183
Gideon's Army 184
Elijah And 450 Prophets Of Baal 186
General Notes 187
Chapter Six: Where To Find Help In Bible For Genuine Success And Prosperity 191
Prayers Of The Bible 194

Introduction

I'm still wondering within me with the way the Holy Spirit of God, my Senor Companion, proceeded to deal with me! I am not ashamed, but I am profoundly humbled to acknowledge that without him, I can do nothing but do all things with him.

Through revelation on key healing Scriptures, faith declarations, inspiring testimonies, prophetic decrees, and healing confessions you will be equipped to break demonic sickness and strongholds that hold back your prosperity and healing.

I thank God for the grace that He has given me to hear Him and follow His voice. I tried faithfully to follow the voice as I was commanded to write this book. I hope that as many as read this book will find spiritual insights that will change their lives for better. In certain instances, only one word is necessary. I hope there are a few such terms in it.

May God alone is glorified when He does what He wants to do in your life, conditions and circumstances if you only wish to allow Him.

Chapter One: Immediate Called

Called From Your Mother's Womb

Jeremiah 1:5 KJV

Before I formed thee in the belly, I know thee, And before thou cometh forth out the womb, I sanctified thee and ordained thee a prophet unto the nations.

The transcendent Creator understood everything that he had made or would have ceased to be God. He has uncreated himself. Therefore, He exercises absolute control over all that He has formed. He knows the tiny things of all His creation, such as the number of hairs on each person's head and weight, breath, colour and every other precise structure of each strand of hair: nobody created has ever chosen their Father or mother. The Almighty decides all. This means that He knows every mother. But every womb and the number of descendants will come from a certain particular womb.

Jeremiah, in the scripture at the beginning of the verse, represents every human being. Thus, even as a speck of matter, God called him and made all the possible qualities appropriate for him to be a prophet to the nations. How unbelievable! Yeah, all the distinctive features of that speck of matter were incorporated in it to distinguish it from billions of others, allowing it to be different in everything he does to extraordinary.

The great news is there was a plan made by God for every human-made, and that plan will be ultimately successful as long as it is implemented according to God's requirements. Not so good news is that free will appears to be constraining for those who like to exercise their freedom of choice. The choice that God gives man is either to pursue Him {to obey His commands} or to deny His commandments} And this is exclusive for the human created in the image of God,   All non - living beings follow God without fail at all times and in all places. That should be the preserve of the Sovereign Creator.

Appropriate allocation:

In reality, there is nothing that God made without intent, from minute to minute, insignificant organism to man, and from curse to galaxies and planets. No human-made in the image of God is worthless or negligible.

There is a particular assignment for every human being, which is why there is no photocopy. Every human being is unique and special to God.

So the initial move is to figure out what our assignment is. It takes humanity to inquire. That's where prayers come in; the weaker must ask from the more vital—the creature of the Lord, the tiny One of the Almighty. A man with a spirit of arrogance as Satan prays because he assumes that he has the same rank as his Creator. How ridiculous it is! How absurd it is! How inane it is! If one acknowledges one's assignment and pursues that assignment diligently, there will be no question of failure, for the criterion of success is God's specification and not man's or world's. That's why it's possible to have a total loss in life; even the world has seen him as a successful person.

Isaiah 55: 7, 8

Let the wicked forsake his way, and the unrighteous man his thoughts and let him return unto the LORD, and He will have mercy upon him: and to our God, He will abundantly pardon. 8. For my thoughts are not your thoughts, neither your ways my ways saith the LORD.

We ought to adhere to the thoughts of God and the ways of God, and as we do so, I assure you that He who is the Author and Finisher of our life, the Planner of Success and Victory, and the Master of Excellence, will lead you to divine success, victory, even as spiritual principles and concepts are unveiled to you in this book. Indeed, God does not respect any individual, race, tribe, ethnicity, age, colour, place, class, or education. Every man who knows the laws of God obeys them and obeys them. Carry them out, will surely make it in this life. God always rewards what He has assigned.

Awareness for calling

God has called every man to Himself. He called Adam, he called Abraham, he named Isaac, he called Jacob, he called Joseph, he called Moses, he called Joshua, and the judges, the prophets who replied. Isaiah said, "Here am I to submit" Isaiah 6:8. In the New Testament, Jesus called the twelve disciples who had already answered.

You may be shocked, but God is calling you, too. He knows your name, just as He revealed it to Isaiah [Isaiah 41:1]. You need to respond to Him. He's calling in the cool, gentle, calm voice. You cannot hear Him in the crowd, in the din, in the clutter, and the confusion of the world. No! No! You will need to be alone to hear His call if you haven't heard Him before. We shall now discuss Peter's call.

Peter's Call

In St. Luke's Gospel, chapter 5: 1 to 11, we locate Jesus and Peter the Galilean from Bathsida by the Lake of Gennesaret. Two exasperated and disappointed fishers. Peter and his brother Andrew had worked all night and caught no fish. They washed their nets to return to their homes when Jesus asked them to lend him their boat to teach and preach to the great crowd that followed.

Just after the message, Jesus asked the fishermen to cast their nets in deeper water for an uncommon catch. They were met by the advice of a novice fisherman, whom they had never seen fishing in those waters before. Nevertheless, they consented to the advice given to him by his word. By the way, He told them to cast their nets in several locations. However, they released only one catch, and yet they entangled so much fish that their boat and the accompanying boat of their friends were almost sinking. Faced with the supernatural {indeed divine} presence, Peter was so bewildered that he knelt before Jesus and worshiped Him, confessing that he was indeed a sinner! Jesus replied.

"Do not be afraid; from now on, you shall catch men.

The Bible is confirmed in Luke 5 vs 11

"As they brought their ships to the shore, they forsook all of them and pursued Him"

We may claim that Peter and Andrew were unsuccessful fishermen. Not only did Jesus, who created fish in His divine nature, teach them how to become successful fishermen, but He also showed to them what a more fabulous dream He had for them to be men's fishers. Even so, like Peter and Andrew, many of us have learned a trade or a career, and we believe that this is our destiny. There may be a need for a career change, as we see in this story. We talk of our vocation {the root in Latin means, by the way, "call" vocare} However, this may not be the correct call of God to us. There can be no real success in life unless one responds to the unique need of God. Let me repeat this, and Heaven always reward what he has assigned. After all, a banker, a lawyer, an engineer, an architect, or an author may never succeed unless he accepts the unique call of God and forsakes all else to obey Jesus as Peter and Andrew. Their friends did and transformed the world, even though they were ordinary uneducated men.

The Greater or Higher Call

Jesus showed Peter and Andrew, and the sons of Zebedee {James and John} who were in the second ship {Matthew 4:21,22} a nobler or higher call. It was not a call to fulfill their own need for subsistence for themselves {their belly if you may} and the members of their families or the few who would buy fish from them, but a higher or nobler call for the hearts of many more men. To endeavour to introduce others to Christ is the mandate of God to all humanity.

It is the heart of God in the Great Commission {Matthew 28:18,19,20}.

It is also the Pauline commission which Jesus gave to Paul, a former fanatical Jew and Pharisee of the Pharisees, a distinguished lawyer who had been educated under the most outstanding Gamaliel, who ended up being called to the Apostle of the Gentiles (Acts:26:16,18).

God, the King, he made men for his enjoyment. God didn't want a commission with only one man. He decided to contribute to all of His development by keeping fellowship with them.

This is an act of pure love for humanity because God's nature is love; selfishness is common to the unbelieving heart of man. However, man reacquires the nature of God; he becomes God's centred and others centred than self-centred. No doubt people gain more satisfaction by doing good to others than from self-centred reasons that cannot be entirely fulfilled, no matter how much material one acquires. It's all in connection to the Creator so that a man can receive full joy and peace.

Also, in the Gospel of John 17, the High Priestly Prayer of Jesus Christ before He went to Calvary for His crucifixion, there are two items which He referred to as the foundations between Him and His Father. They are the glory of Heaven, the love of God. Jesus' prayer was like a farewell, and we can gain from it a few insights into the success of life because He is the most outstanding example of human success, the fulfillment of His Father's perfect will.

According to vs 4 and 5, we read:

"I have glorified thee on the earth: I have finished the work which thou gavest me to do: and now, O Father, glorify me with thy own self with the glory which I had with thee before the world was."

In verse 24, we see

Father, I will that they also, whom thou has given Me, be with Me where I am, that they may behold My glory which thou hast given Me for thou lovest Me before the foundational of the world."

In verse 26, we read:

"And I have declared unto them thy name, and will deliver it: that the love wherewith thou hast loved me may be in them and I in them."

And what's the glory of the Lord?

The glory of God is the representation of the presence of God, Divine light, His unfathomable light, His insatiable fire, His majesty,

His magnificence, His majesty, His perfection, His righteousness, His perfection, His supremacy, His greatness, as manifested in the face of Moses, as He received the commandments in the pillar of cloud by day, and the pillars of fire by night, to accompany the people of God.

The majesty of God was represented as a dove during the baptism of Jesus Christ and as a very bright light on the Mount of Transfiguration. The glory of God was fully manifested in

Jesus Christ and, therefore, should be expressed in the lives of true believers. Indeed, the basic qualities and characteristics of God are His glory, which we should also pursue. This is a contract with the glory of man, which appears to be his apparent strength, authority, or wealth and belongings.

The glory of mankind is not a weak shadow of the unparalleled, unsurpassed and unprecedented glory of God. If our purpose is to pursue the glory of God in every move and operation, we shall surely attain success and prosperity beyond all comprehension.

Love of the Lord

The love of God {Hesed in Hebrew and Agape in Greek} is the ultimate essence of God and the most potent force of existence. It is translated as loving-kindness: "compassion" and can mean profound loyalty to others or deep concern for the needs of others. It contrasts with human love, which means a passionate, lustful desire for a person of the opposite sex. God's love is independent of every man's acts or needs. The higher call of God makes a man love even his enemies. The love of God to mankind is so powerful that He gave His only begotten Son to die in place of man.

John 3:16

For God so love the world He gave His only begotten Son, whosoever believed Him should not perish but have everlasting life.

Love As a Higher Call

Read what the scriptures say about love:

Proverbs 10:12

"Hatred stirreth up strife, but love covereth all sins."

1 Peter 4:8

"And above all things have fervent charity {LOVE} among yourself: for your charity shall cover a multitude of sins.

Romans 13: 8and 12

Own no man anything, but love one another, for he that loveth another had fulfilled the law. Love worketh no ill to his neighbour: therefore love is the fulfilling of the law.

1 Corinthians 13: 1 to 13

"Though I speak with the tongues of men and of angels, and have not charity, I am becoming a sounding brass or a thinking cymbal.

And though I have the gift of prophecy, and though I have all mysteries and all knowledge, and though I have all faith, so that I can remove mountains, and have not charity, I a nothing.

And though I bestow all my goods to feed the poor, and though I give my body to be burned, and have no charity, it profits me nothing.

Charity suffereth long and is kind, charity envieth not, charity vaunteth not itself, it is not puffed up, Does not behave itself unseemly, seeketh not her own is not easily provoked, thinketh no evil.

Rejoiceth not in iniquity, but rejoiceth in the truth. Beareth all things. Believeth all things, hopeth all things, endureth all things.

Charity never faileth, but whether there be prophesies, they shall fail: whether there be tongues they shall cease, whether there be knowledge they shall vanish away.

For we know in part, and we prophesy in part. But when that which is perfect has come, then that which is in part shall be done away.

When I was a child, I speak as a child, I thought like a child, but when I became a man. I put away childish things. For now, we see through a glass darkly but then face to face.

Now I know in parts, but then shall I know even as also I am known. And now abideth faith, hope, charity, these three, but the greatest of these is charity.

SUMMARY

In summary, we have studied the distinctive call of every man that God made. God loves everyone dearly and would desire that each know his own unique calling to make sense to each life. A positive response to God's call guarantees progress and perfection, based on God's own ideal, not on any earthly standard. There is a higher call that seeks the benefit of others above self. It is focused on finding the glory of God and is empowered by completely undeserved love and deep passion for mankind. This will motivate a man to love God and also love One another according to the scriptures, in order to gain heavenly rewards.

Prayer Points For My Family

- *Father, in the name of Jesus, today I thank you for the redemption of my soul.*
- *Father, in the name of Jesus, I thank you because you have heard me before I say these prayer points for my family.*
- *Father, in the name of Jesus, I thank you for having fought my battles at the cross of Calvary.*

- *I'm freeing myself from any household slavery in my family.*
- *The fire of the living God, like you, came down in the days of Elijah, consuming every chain of poverty, addiction, injustice, and failure in my life today. Kings 18:38*
- *Holy Ghost Fire, just as the days of Elisha sent mysterious animals to destroy any agent who kept my finances and the finances of my family. Two Kings 2:23-24.*

- *Heavenly Father, when the sea opened, engulfed the enemies of your people who had held them, prisoner, for years. Let the sea swallow any ancestral spirit that has kept my family bond.*
- *Let the powerful arm of God that broke the chains of Paul and Silas in the prison break any chain that binds me to my past and prevents me from the future God has prepared for my family and me. Laws 16:25-34.*

- *Heavenly Father, as you rescued Daniel and the three Hebrew children from the hands of their oppressors, deliver my family and me from the slavery of poverty, suffering, and failure. Daniel 6:1-28, please.*
- *Nuclear warheads from the heavenly places begin to bomb every coven in which the glory of my family is concealed.*
- *Intermittent rockets begin to fall on every cage where the fate of my family is held.*

- *This year, every strong person from my father's home, or every evil Personality from my mother's side, who imprisoned me in a room of failure, would open the doors and be dishonored in the name of Jesus. Matthew 12:29 p.m.*
- *Hailstones and fire from above begin to fall on any philistine who has kidnapped, tortured, and broken the finances of my helpers today. Joshua 10:11 a.m.*

Command Your Destiny

Chapter Two: Designing and Building:

JOSHUA 1: 6

Be strong and of good courage, for unto this people shalt thou divide for an inheritance the Land which I swore unto their fathers to give them.

Designing and Building {Commissioning} is a mandate given to a man to carry out an assignment on behalf of God. God's assignments differ from one man to another; even the place of assignment may also differ. If you have studied God's assignment to Moses, the whole thing was like a drama, the way He appeared to him on a burning bush. God can decide to commission someone through an angel or a person He has appointed, as happened in the case of Moses and Joshua; the reason is that God always wants to equip the person He has appointed in order to achieve the mandate of the specific assignment. God works through such individual;

no wonder every assignment from God always succeed.

Let's see how Moses was commission.

Moses

Moses kept his father-in-law's flock, Jethro, in the backwoods of the Midan Desert on Mount Horeb when the angel of the Lord unexpectedly appeared to him in a mysterious fire in a bush that was apparently burning, but the bush was not consumed. In his curiosity, Moses turned to look at the unusual sight.

Then, out of the flames, God spoke his name to him. There was no premonition. It was a common humdrum day on which Moses had gone to perform his Shepherd duties as before, after about 40years. Having declared that the Land where Moses stood was sacred, God revealed to Moses that he was the God of Abraham, Isaac, and Jacob.

That he had learned the afflictions of the children of Israel under their Egyptian slave masters, that he was able to release them from the house of slavery, he requested Moses to go to Pharaoh to make the deliverance a reality.

Emotion puzzled, unsure, unworthy, and inferior, Moses declined the commission stressing his inadequacies. Earlier the prince in the trial of Pharaoh deliverer to his brothers and failed painfully, ending in his beating a strategic exit to the Midian 40 years earlier, what a change for a man educated in Egyptian law, military and royal traditions now trained as a shepherd in modesty and endurance in a daily company of mere sheep.

Exodus 3:12

And God said: Certainly I will be with thee and this shall be a token unto thee, that I have sent thee: when thou hath brought forth the people out of Egypt, ye shall serve God upon this mountain.

God introduced Himself to Moses.

Exodus 3:14 and 15

I AM THAT I AM: and He said, Thus shalt thou say unto the children of Israel, I AM THAT I AM, hath sent me unto you. This is my name forever, and this is my memorial unto all generations.

Since Moses was still in question, God showed him the strength that he had bestowed upon Moses. He asked Moses to put the rod on the ground. The rod was turned into a serpent that Moses had fled from there. God asked Moses to pick up the serpent by the tail. As Moses obeyed, the serpent was transformed back into a rod. God asked Moses to lay his hand in his chest. As he did, his hand became leprous like snow. God ordered him to bring the leprous hand back on his chest again. When Moses brought out his hand, it was normal and fresh. God went further and said to Moses, in case these two signs did not convince the people of Israel, take some water from the river and pure it on the dry Land; it will turn to blood.

When Moses was still complaining about his difficulties in speaking, God told him that He would be with Moses' mouth, and God knew that Moses' elder brother was eloquent, and God promised to make Aaron available to support him by empowering Aaron's mouth and making Moses like God to Aaron. However, Moses was to take his shepherd's rod, which would be used to make signs and wonders in Egypt.

The summary is that, if God would send anyone, He will definitely equip the person to achieve or accomplish the commission.

Joshua

Joshua was a loyal and devoted servant to Moses. When God had agreed that Moses would no longer lead the children of Israel to the Promised Land, he asked Moses for the appointment to the Joshua Commission.

"And the LORD said unto Moses, Look, thy days come, that thou mayest die: call Joshua, and set thyself in the temple of the synagogue, that I may give him charge; Moses and Joshua went and stood in the tabernacle of the congregation; and the LORD came close unto him in the temple in a pillar of a cloud and pillar of cloud stood over the synagogue { Deuteronomy 3: 14 and 15}

Deuteronomy 34:9

"And Joshua the son of Nun was full of the Spirit of wisdom: for Moses had laid his hand

upon him, and the children of Israel hearkened unto him and did as the Lord commanded Moses.

Moses, my servant is dead: now, therefore, arise go over this Jordan, thou, and this entire people, unto the Land which I do give to them, even to the children of Israel.

Every place that the Soul of thy foot shall tread upon that have I given unto you, as I said unto Moses

From the Wilderness and this Lebanon even unto the great river, the river Euphrates, all the Land of Hittites, and unto the great sea toward the going down of the sun, shall be your coast.

There shall not any man be able to stand before thee all the days of thy life. As I was with Moses, so I will be with thee: I will not fail thee nor forsake thee.

Be strong and of good courage: for unto this people shall thou divide for an inheritance the Land which I swore un their Father to give them.

Only be thou strong and very courageous: that thou mayest observe to do according to the law: which Moses my servant commanded thee: "turn not from it to the right hand or to the left, that thou mayest prosper wheresoever thou goest.

This book of the law shall not depart out of the mouth. But thou shall meditate therein day and night. That thou mayest observe to do according to all that is written therein for then thou shall make your way prosperous, and then thou shall have good success.

Have not I commanded thee? Be strong and of good courage: be not afraid, neither be thou dismay for the Lord thy God is with thee wheresoever thou goest.

Joshua 1:2 to 9

The biblical requirements for true success and prosperity in life are as follows;

Strength, courage, diligence these three things that can be achieved when someone puts his trust and confidence in God.

Meditating on the word of God day and night

Fellowshipping with God always.

He was hearkening to the voice of God by dwelling in His divine presence.

By the way, Joshua was one of the two spies {the other was Caleb} of the twelve spies that Moses had sent to view the Promised Land, who had returned with a positive report that they were able to take the Land, unlike the unfaithful, doubting ten who said there was a giant in the Land that they were like grasshoppers in comparison. There's no way a grasshopper can conquer a giant. We need more than that mindset to be champions and overcomers. No wonder those who have evil reports were not able to enter the Promised Land. Certainly, many of them who were above 20 years of age who had that evil report could not enter the Promised Land; they died in the Wilderness. Joshua and Caleb, with those with strong faith, successfully entered the Promised Land and possessed it with the good things the Lord had promised their fathers Abraham, Isaac and Jacob.

Isaiah

Isaiah, a very well-educated, well-begotten son of high-class Jerusalem Jews, called Amoz, was a man who mixed up with the royal but was not afraid to speak the word of God. He was married to the prophetess and blessed with two sons. He himself had a prophetic gift. It was after King Uzziah's death that Isaiah saw the image of the Lord in glorious glory seated on a throne high up in the sanctuary. There were Seraphim {angelic beings sparkling like burning fire, which means purity and holiness} that covered all over the temple.

Holy, Holy, Holy, is the Lord of the host the whole earth is full of His glory. The temple was filled with smoke as the doorpost shifted. According to Isaiah, he was so afraid when he saw that vision.

Woe is me, for I am undone, because I am a man unclean lips, and I dwell in the midst of people of unclean lips, for my eyes have seen the King, the Lord of a host.{Isaiah 6:3 to 5}

Certainly, seeing God was unfathomable in the natural universe. That would have contributed to his death. One of the Seraphim, therefore, used a string to pick up a hot piece of coal that he put in Isaiah's mouth to purge his sin and purify it.

When Isaiah heard the voice of God saying:

Whom shall I send, and who will go for us? Isaiah responded: Here am I Father send me" { Isaish 6:8}

And God said:

Go and tell these people, Hear ye indeed, but perceive not.

Make the heart of these people fat, and make their ears heavy,

And shut their eyes, lest they see with the eyes and hear with their ears,

And understand with their heart, and convert and be healed. {Isaiah 6:10}

This was to take place until the towns had been abandoned, and the entire Land had become absolutely barren. There would, however, be a tiny remnant of the people who would believe and be preserved. This would be the new Judah in which God would carry out His plan of salvation not only for the Jews but also for the entire human race. They will be loyal, faithful and holy to the Lord, absolutely obedient to His word and enjoy eternity in His presence.

Jeremiah

Jeremiah "s call happened when he was still small; God called him. As he was complaining to God about his incompetence, God told him that before he was born, right from his mother's womb, He knew whom he would become, that he should not bother about his inadequacies; God called Jeremiah as a Prophet. He told him not to be afraid that He the Lord would be with him to accomplish the assignment. God promised to speak through his mouth to command the people without compromise.

"Be not afraid for I am with thee to deliver thee, saith the Lord" {Jeremiah 1:8}

According to Jeremiah's vision, he saw when God was anointing his lips for an assignment.

"see I have this day set the over the nations and over the kingdoms to root out and to pull down, and to destroy, throw down, to build and to plant."{Jeremiah 1:10}

This is to say that Jeremiah's commission includes both Judgments {the main concept of the Old Testament} and Salvation { the main concept of the New Testament}.

The message that Jeremiah brought was, however, more biased forward into judgment in the face of the insurrection of the people he was speaking to. Jeremiah's time was during the reigns of five kings {from Josiah to Zedekiah} At that time, the nation of the {Southern Kingdom} was in great rebellion against the commandments of God and relied heavily on alliances with other kingdoms to fight the enemy, and Jeremiah's message of warning against sins and the need for of reconciliation was controversial and therefore ineffective, and for that reason, Jeremiah suffered great persecution.

God further gave Jeremiah the vision of an almond tree, usually the first tree to bud in the spring. This was to prove that what God revealed to the prophet would manifest quickly. And that it was the completion of God's plan and intent in history.

Second, God gave the prophet a boiling pot with steam pointing toward the North Land. This meant that there would be an invasion of Jerusalem by the Northern enemy {Babylon} as a result of the apostasy and idol worship of the people, gods who were not helping them.

When God discovered that prophet Jeremiah was speaking the word to the kings without fear, He promised to be with him and to back him up with courage and boldness. God did this to make sure that their persecutions and rebellion would not overcome the prophet. God had never failed to rescue or be with

Jeremiah. Later, Jeremiah became the most intelligent and most popular prophet nationwide. And all the kings were seeking his counsel.

The Great Commission

Jesus introduced this commission to His disciples after His death and resurrection. Initially, He requested that they must receive the power of the Holy Spirit to enable them to spread the gospel to all nations. As they waited in Jerusalem at the Upper Room, when the time came, they all received the power of the

Holy Spirit, and immediately they began to speak in different tongues and yet they understood themselves in various languages.

This is where we received the commission of Jesus:

Matthew 28: 18 to 20

And Jesus came and spoke to them saying, all power is given unto me in Heaven and in the earth. Go ye therefore, and teach all nations, baptizing them in the name of the

Father, and of the Son, and of the Holy Ghost.

Teaching them to observe all things whatsoever I have commanded you: and behold, I am with you always, even the end of this word. Amen

Acts 1:8

But ye shall receive power, after that. Holy Ghost has come upon you: and ye shall be witnesses unto me both in Jerusalem, and in all Judea, and in Samaria, and unto the uttermost part of the earth.

Certainly, these promises were fulfilled as they assembled at the upper room in one accord on the day of Pentecost.

Acts 2: 2 to 4

And suddenly there came a sound from Heaven as of the rushing of a mighty wind, and it filled all the house where they were sitting.

And there appeared unto them cloven tongues like of fire, and it sat upon each of them.

And they were all filled with the Holy Ghost and began to speak with other tongues, as the Spirit gave them utterance.

In our individual assignments, God had not left us empty-handed. He has made the Holy Spirit available for us to accompany us to achieve great commission. It is our responsibility to seek the Holy Spirit, who is our best teacher, comforter, counsellor, and senior partner, for, without him, we can do nothing. The gospel of Jesus Christ is for every creature to reconcile humanity with God; whoever believes after confession and repentance would be baptized. With this, we are made whole physically, emotionally, economically, materially, and spiritually with an abundance of peace and joy.

CONCLUSION:

In summary, we have read about the four men whom God commissioned {Moses, Joshua, Isaiah, Jeremiah,} and also the disciples of Jesus Christ. The good news is they were all empowered by God to accomplish the assignment. In the same manner, God has not to stop nor changed in His calling. He is still calling us today; you need to pay attention to His call for a successful future.

Like the disciples of Jesus, God has given everyone a specific assignment and great commission to go to the world and preach the gospel to every creature, and He has empowered you for this assignment.

Chapter Three: Trust in the Lord

Trust in the Lord with all thine heart and lean not unto thine understanding. In all thy ways acknowledge Him, and He shall direct thy part". {Proverbs 3: 5,6}

Faith consists of confidence and absolute trust in God: trust in Him and the certainty and utter assurance that He will deliver or do whatever

He says He will do. Man's answer is confidence, devotion, obedience to God.

Of course, God remains absolutely reliable trustworthy and trustworthy because He is all-powerful, He knows all things, and He is present everywhere at the same time. He doesn't rely on anyone because he wasn't made.

Before the formation, he was in the universe. He will remain after all that He has made perishes. It's absolutely unrestricted by dimensions, time or room. It is beyond any kind of human categorization and understanding. Any level of excellence can be driven only by His standard.

There is a tendency, through ordinary human experience, not to accept what one cannot see. Unfortunately, this is the uniqueness of the Christian religion. It does not rely on normal human sensations or feelings. It depends entirely on God, who is unseen, and yet beyond lies. The Scriptures prove that no one can see God and live. {Exodus 33, 20}.

This remains an expectation for those who have overcome or are good in this earthly existence. No man has ever seen in His real appearance, of Jesus Christ reveal Himself as the almighty God.

John 1:14

"And the word was made flesh, and dwelth among us { and we behold Hid glory, the glory of the only begotten son of the Father} full of grace and truth."

When one of Jesus' disciples, Philip, asked, how can we know the Father?

Jesus answered and said: Have I be with you and yet had not known me, Philip? He that had seen me had seen the Father, and how sayest thou, then show us the Father? Believest thou, not that. Are I in the Father and the Father in me? The word that I speak unto you, I speak not of myself: but the Father that dwelleth in me, He doeth the works. Believe me that I am in the Father and the Father in me. {John 14: 9 to 11}

Belief

Belief is at the heart of every faith. Men prefer to believe whatever they want to believe. Belief should be focused on the facts, which should not be modified. Belief should be founded on honesty; the quality that says yes is yes, no is no, white is white, black is black. It's not like sinking sand or quicksilver. It's a solid rock. In other words, we should be sure about the object by which we place our confidence, our religion, or our faith. After all, every relationship needs to be built on trust or honesty; such a friendship will collapse.

The originality of the Religion of Christ

Jesus Christ is the object of faith in God since God has revealed Himself to man through Him. From the historical proof of His birth, crucifixion, death and resurrection, Jesus is the cornerstone of the Christian religion. Indeed, no other hinges on his doctrine of the redemption of sin and the need of human response {calling for the Savior} What would be the need for rules, ordinances, practices, rites, rituals or sacrifices if they do not bring change that will make meaning to human life?

Life would be pointless if it weren't for any good, no reason. Purpose becomes realizable when there is a path, the reality is there, and the end is understood. Jesus categorically instructed the disciple, Philip.

"I am the Way, the Truth and the Life. No man cometh to the Father, but by me". John 14:6

What we are saying is that if one puts one's faith, confidence or belief in a religion, ideology, theory or human being or thing, One does so in vain.

How Does The Scripture Define Faith?

Hebrews 11:1 to 3

"Now, faith is the substance of things hoped for, the evidence of things not seen. For by it elders obtained a good report. Through faith, we understand that the worlds were framed by the word of God so that things which are seen were not made of things which do appear.

What it simply means is that you can claim whatsoever you need from God by faith; you assume that those things are already with you. Through faith, you possess things, and they become yours. There is assurance; there is a certainty. The scripture says the elders received a good report; in other words, they were successful. Because of their faith, they received from God and excelled in what they were doing. There is so much confidence, hope and trust in the word of God. God cannot deny Himself because the word of God is God Himself.

John 1:1 to 3

"In the beginning was the word, and the word was with God, and the word was God. The same was in the beginning with God. All things were made by Him. And without Him was not anything made that was made".

Abraham is our role model; he believed God's promise at the age of 100 years that he would bear a son.

Likewise, his wife, who has passed the age of menopause {at 90 years} yet the promise of bearing Isaac was made to her by God. Even when the promise of bearing Isaac came to manifestation, Abraham trusted God by obeying his instruction of sacrificing Isaac to him. Abraham did not hesitate to do what God asked him to do until a Lamb was provided for the sacrifice, and God counted it for him as righteousness. {Genesis 15:6}

Likewise, Moses, who believed and trusted God when he was assigned to deliver the Israelites from Pharaoh in Egypt. He overlooked the tile and pleasures from Pharaoh and embarked on delivering his brethren without seeing God. And God proved Himself at the red sea by allowing Pharaoh and all his soldiers and horsemen to perish at the red sea.

Noah trusted and obeyed God when he was instructed to build an ark. This instruction was given. As a result of immoralities and wickedness going on during that period. The world was destroyed, Noah and his household were delivered {Genesis 6:6}

How about Rahab the harlot, the ancestress of our Lord Jesus Christ through Obed and Booz. A woman who sheltered two spies sent by Joseph to Jericho. Rabab believed so much in the God of Israelites; even when the wall of Jericho was devastated by supernatural power, she was rescued because she trusted the God of Israelites.

Faith Prays to Heaven

God has produced man for His enjoyment. Indeed, a good man must satisfy his maker, for he will rejoice in the things he does. Without faith, it is impossible to please God who is a rewarder of those who delight seek Him {Hebrew 11:6}

Success In Life Is Dependent On Trusting God

According to the book of Proverbs where we read earlier, Proverbs 3:5,6, We are ordered to trust in the Lord with all our hearts. What it means is to believe in and rely entirely on God. That would be the wisest choice since God is trustworthy in every way. To doubt or disbelieve, God is to question His incomparable dignity. People who appear to rely on themselves, others, or their abilities have completely missed it. God demands and expects us to depend entirely on Him, even as little children depend on their parents for everything. Indeed, God says that we should come to Him as little children, for He is a father to all that seek Him in that manner. The book of Proverbs demanded that we must acknowledge God in everything we do, so He can direct our paths. This may sound so easy. The truth is that the more we depend on our human understanding, the more we are far from God. Another important thing is that we must humble ourselves before God so He would elevate us to a greater height. God rebukes the proud and gives grace to the humble. God is way, and He knows all the paths; when we follow Him, He will direct our paths, and success would be achieved.

The Just Shall Live By Faith

Habakkuk 2:4

"Behold, his Soul, which is lifted up, is not upright in him, but the just shall live by faith.

The reward of true righteousness or faith in God is internal life, which comes through the belief we have in our Lord Jesus Christ.

{John 3:36}

"He that believeth in the Son hath everlasting life: and that believeth not in the Son shall not see life: but the wrath of God abideth in him.

1 John 5: 11,12

Father: "And this is the record that God hath given to us eternal life, and this life is in the Son. He that hath the Son hath life: and he that hath not the Son of God hath not life.

This is a serious allegation against those who do not believe in Jesus Christ. The BibleBible claims there's no life. It means they're living dead bodies. They're unprofitable to God. Jesus told the unbeliever to Thomas, who focused on seeing the nail prints on His hand when He appeared to them after His crucifixion.

John 20:29

"Thomas, because thou hath seen me, thuo hath believed: blessed are they that hath not seen, and yet have believed."

Walk By Faith, Not By Sight

A lot of people in the world are like Thomas's unbelievers. They need to see this before they can believe it. This is living in the real, that is, "seeing is believing," which sounds rational on the surface; Jesus says, blessed are those who believe without seeing. Indeed, this is the spiritual high point, contrary to the natural world view or outlook. If one's confidence is in Christ, then one can see the unseen and do the impossible. Man's natural eyes are grossly restricted, as we see in the story of Elisha asking God to open the eyes of his servant, Gehazi, who was deeply worried that the Syrian army was about to overpower his Master. Prophet Elisha prayed, and God opened the eyes of Gehazi, who saw an enormous army of horses and chariots encircling Elisha, and then the enemy was defeated. {2 Kings 6: 15 to 18}

God really wants us to have faith so we can operate in the spiritual realm, to enable us to see some invisible things.

The woman of Samaria had a mindset that it was only in Jerusalem temple that God was to be worshipped. Jesus disagreed with her saying:

{John 4:24} "God is Spirit and they that worship Him, must worship Him in spirit and in truth."

God can be worshiped anywhere, any time, any location, every time. God has also created man to have the body of a soul, and the Spirit of God the Head is made up of three identities, the Father, the Son, and the Holy Spirit. Man's Spirit is man's true nature, which can be linked to the Spirit of God. In order for man to function to his maximum potential, he needs to operate in the spirit realm. A man who works in his body operates in the flesh: he operates by sight. If we function in the Spirit, we are operating by faith. The Spirit and the flesh does not agree with each other at all time. We can only be successful when we allow the Spirit to overcome the flesh in whatsoever we are doing. This is what Apostle Paul says in the book of:

{Galatians 5:16,17} This I say then, walk in the Spirit, and ye shall not fulfill the lust of the flesh. For the flesh lusteth against the Spirit and the Spirit against the flesh: and these are contrary to one another: so that ye cannot do the things that ye would."

In order words, walking in the flesh may lead to death, while walking in Spirit will lead to everlasting life.

Benefit Of Faith In Christ

One of the benefits of faith in Christ is the reward of entering Heaven and having eternal life. This is the ultimate plan of God for man. Enter Heaven, and eternal life is the greatest victory that every man should pray to achieve. Faith in Christ gives confidence and not pride. Jesus said to His disciples, and there shall be no impossibility to him that believes. { Mark 9:23}

Faith in Christ opens the avenue for the gift of the Holy Spirit, our senior partner, the source of comfort, love, power, joy, peace, patience, goodness, gentleness, kindness, faithfulness and self-control.

Faith in Christ gives us peace during the time of trials and persecutions, and sufferings.

Faith in Christ helps to build and transform our lives from ordinary to extraordinary, successful, excellent persons pleasing God at all times.

CONCLUSION:

In summary, faith in Christ is the cornerstone of Christian doctrine. Jesus Christ is trustworthy and has total honesty. When we trust Him and recognize Him with all our Heart, Soul and mind, he's committed to giving us the win. Faith is pleasing to God; Faith is an overcomer. Confidence is mighty. When we walk by faith and not by sight, we walk in the Spirit and thus shun the flesh. The Spirit brings life, and the flesh brings death. When we confess what we believe from the word of God, we receive what we confess. Speaking out what we desire with confidence and boldness without a doubt in our heart, in as much it's according to the perfect will of God, will amount to great success. Words are powerful more, especially scriptural declaration. Always practice faith because, without faith, it is impossible to please God.

Chapter Four Prosperity Is the Will Of God

Beloved, I wish above all things that thou mayest prosper and be in health even as your soul prosperity. [3 John: 1 2}

From the beginning, in the Garden of Eden, God created man to have dominion over all the creatures of the earth. Man was enjoying without lacking anything until man sinned against God. Assuming man did not sin against God, he would have maintained his authority over all the birds, the fish, the animals, the Land, the sea, and all cripple things of the world. {Genesis: 1: 8} Because of disobedient man was subjected to the judgment of sin which denied him of the intended prosperity God had offered him at the beginning. And that was why Jesus told His disciple when He was teaching them the Lord's Prayer.

He said..... "Thy kingdom come thy will be done on earth as it is in Heaven." {Matthew 6:10}

This means, when praying, we should ask or desire to have the good things of this life which God had already made available for us in Heaven to locate us. The good mansion, cars, success, victory, etc.

The Lord's Prayer is the summary of every prayer we want to pray, especially when it comes to making a request from GOD.

In Matthew 7:7 to 8

"Ask and it shall be given to you, seek, and ye shall find: knock and it shall be opened unto you: for every one that asketh recieveth: and he that seeketh findeth: and to him that knocketh: it shall be opened."

Verse 11 " If ye then, being evil, know how to give good gift to your children, how much more shall your Father which is in heaven give good things to them that ask Him?"

God Is always faithful when it comes to promises and covenant. He never fails to fulfill His words and promises.

Number 23:19

"God is not a man, that He should lie, neither the son of man that He should repent: He had not said and shall not make it happen."

What Is The Will Of God?

The will of God may mean the revealed guidance of God to man expressed in His laws in the commandments and in the whole Word of God. It can also mean the intention or purpose of God for mankind. This is often referred to as the Perfect Will of God. Since he never wanted anyone to perish, that all might come to the knowledge of God and receive salvation {2 Peter 3:9, 1 Timothy 2:4}

Thirdly, there is the permissive will of God, which reflects what God allows to happen temporarily in the hands of Satan in the universe as a result of man's sin in the Garden of Eden. Thus God wrenches the authority of Satan at the final judgment, sins of suffering abuse, hate, lust may continue even though these are not the wishes of God but of a man who has submitted himself to the lordship of sin and Satan. God has given man the power to make choices, and as long as man makes choices that are contrary to the perfect will of God, some sins and evil will not stop on earth. However, God is always sovereign over all the results of the universe and may undo any evil that He so desires. And that's ultimately going to be the case as He takes all aspects to excellence.

Jesus Christ is the ideal man who has never sinned all his life in spite of his undeserved and unmerited persecutions, which have never been mirrored or exemplified. He endeavoured to do the will of His Father, and said in His scripture that His meat was to do the will of His Father {John 4:34} Of a truth, Jesus passed through terrible persecutions on the Cross of Calvary, He was tortured until He seated and dropped His blood.

Yet He prayed for the will of the Father to be done:

"Father, if thou be willing, remove this cup from me: Nevertheless not my will but thine be done" {Luke 22:42}

Man, therefore, strives for success and excellence in life to pray and to desire the perfect will of God in all decisions.

Of a truth, God really wants man to prosper:

3 John 1:2

"Beloved, I wish above all things that thou mayest prosper and be in health, even as thy soul prospereth."

Sadly, prosperity preachers have confounded what is obviously a sound doctrine of the complete gospel of Jesus Christ and the perfect will of God to mean the accumulation of riches and material possession as the main focus of Christianity, and have continued to preach and practice their distorted visions nausea. In order to sanitize society, this deserves to be placed in a proper context.

What Is True Prosperity?

Prosperity talks of trying to make life a success or achieving one's strategic goals: to walk victoriously in one's calling: to be a winner in the race of life, or to do good, as others would suggest. When God created the heavens and the earth, He bestowed goodness upon His works.

In Genesis 1:25

"And God made the beast of the earth after his kind, and cattle after their kind, and everything that creepeth upon the earth after hid kind, and God saw that it was good."

And when we read further, after the creation of man, read what happed:

In Genesis 1:31a

"And God saw everything that he had made, and behold, it was very good."

This speaks of a rather successful success in the man-creation enterprise. If His existence was fine and excellent, why should any man in life be a failure or a failure? Clearly, this could not have been the result of the success of the Father Himself.

Money or a means of trade is needed to make life a success, as it will allow one to acquire things and also to pay for the service that one needs to make one successful. Solomon, the richest man who has ever lived, says:

"For wisdom is a defense, and money is defense"{Ecclesiastes 7:12a} and

"A feast is made for laughter: and wine maketh merry, but money answereth all things" {Ecclesiastes 10:19}

However, Apostle Paul emphasized that:

"For the love of money is the root of all evil"{1 Timothy 6:10}

The Rich Young Ruler

How about this story that Jesus Christ shared with His disciples concerning a rich young ruler who met Jesus to inquire what someone could do to have eternal life? Initially, Jesus was telling him to obey the commandments, but the man replied and said: He has tried as much as possible to keep all the laws. Jesus said to him: since have done all these, now go and sell you have your riches and share the money with the poor. Instantly, this man's countenance changed, and he was very sorrowful because he had great riches.

Hear what Jesus replied:

"How difficult shall they that have riches to enter into the Kingdom of God. For it is easier for a camel to go through a needle's eye than a rich man to enter into the Kingdom of God. " {Luke 18:24,25}

The nation of the Pharisees and the common view at that time was that wealth meant great blessing from

God and that the wealthy were sure candidates for heavenly dwelling with God. By responding, Jesus firmly rejected the view.

"The things which are impossible with men are impossible with God." Luke 18:27

In verse 28, Peter said:

"Lo, we have left all and followed you.

And Jesus answered:

"Verily I say unto you, there is no that left his house, or patent, or brethren, or wife, or children for the Kingdom of God's sake, who shall not receive manifold more in this present time. And in the world to come life everlasting. "{Luke 18:29,30}

The Parable Of The Rich Fool {Luke 12:13 to 21}

Previously, there was a disagreement between the two brothers over dividing their inheritance. One of them begged Jesus to interfere. Jesus resisted and warned against covetousness, stressing that life did not consist mainly of an accumulation of worldly possessions. He followed the parable of the wealthy fool who, seeing that he had a great harvest, wanted to create a new and larger barn to store all his fruits and goods. He was also gloating about his purchase, as he said.

"And I say unto my soul, Soul, and thou hast many goods laid up for many years: take thine ease, eat, drink and be merry verse 19

"But God said unto him, thou fool, this night thy Soul shall be required of thee: then whose shall those thing be, which thou had provided. So is he that layeth up treasure for himself., and is no rich toward God". Verse 20 and 21

This underlines how fleeting and unreliable earthly possessions are. No one is bringing something into the world, and no one is leaving carrying any items. They're in their hand as they leave. This case of the rich and beggar, Lazarus in chapter 16: 19, 31, teaches how the worldly endowed ended up in hellfire, while his neighbour begged for crumbs, which had even been rejected from the rich man's table, ended up in Abraham's bosom in Paradise. Wealth was obviously not and is not a passport to Heaven.

Spiritual Aspect for Prosperity

The argument we are making is that prosperity is not just material. Indeed, there are many facets of success that are spiritual.

God's Presence

Moses told God that if God did not accompany them, they would not go out or clash with their enemies. Divine Involvement is extremely necessary for any undertaking. We can do nothing without God, but we can do all things with God. God is the host's captain. Without His interference, no fight can be successful. He's never lost a fight; he's never going to lose a battle. He created the enemy; he created the weapons of war. If God is with us, who can be against us? {Rom. 8:31b}

Divine Favor

If one enjoys the blessing of God, one cannot be refused. For example, God gave favour to the children of Israel in the sight of the Egyptians before they left Egypt, so much so that they borrowed silver and gold jewels from neighbours, and Pharaoh allowed them to leave after 430 years of slave labour. {Exodus 11:1 to 3} It was God's blessing to Esther that the King had not ordered her immediate death because she had confronted him out of season. Even though the

BibleBible did not mention God specifically {Esther 5:1,2}

The Unity of God (Shalom)

Peace, which passes beyond all human understanding, is part of the fruit of the Spirit {Galatians 5:22} and also part of the redemptive plan {Isaiah 53:5} without which there can be no fulfilment or victory in life or any sort of development whatsoever.

The Psalmist has said:

Psalms 37:37

"Mark the ideal man, and behold the upright man, for the end of that man is peace."

Peace is denied to the unrighteous or the bad One.

"But the wicked are like the troubled sea, when it cannot rest, whose waters cast up marine and dirt. There is no peace saith my God to the wicked. {Isaiah 57:20,21}

Divine Health

Even the world appreciates that health is wealth; in other words, wealth without health is illusory and vain. Many rich people are burdened with chronically crippling illnesses that cannot be cured with their income. It is only when one is safe that one can follow the rich since sickness issues can fully overtake any objective endeavour. Jesus Christ is the only man's healer. (Exodus 15:26) And He makes man whole.

The joy of the Lord

The joy of the Lord gave power to Nehemiah as he set out to restore the wall of Jerusalem. {Nehemiah 8:10}

Many rich people have no joy. They may have a brief time of pleasure, but there is no true joy that links the presence of God. In spite of lack, want, and sufferings, joy can be experienced with Jesus Christ and the Holy Spirit. Eighty percent of rich men have become depressed and reclusive, sufferings from phobias of different types. They cannot boast of enjoying life completely.

God's Security {Divine Protection}

Despite the huge increase in human security resources in the walls, electrified barbed wires, bulletproof cars and vest security devices, and so on, many rich people are most insecure.

The Psalmist said:

"Except the Lord build a house, they labour in vain that build it: except the Lord keep the city, the watchman watchet but in vain" [Psalm 127:1}

Admittedly, true protection can only be achieved by the One who has made all things and can be in all places at all times {Omnipresent}: is all immense {Omnipotent} is all-knowing {Omniscient} that there is nothing else but the Almighty Jehovah, the Highest God.

A truly prosperous man, apart from the above, exudes contentment. In spite of the conditions, there is no shortage and no desire. They completely put all their faith and trust in God: not in themselves, their money, their relations, or in some person or thing or entity {other gods}. They are able to adjust to all conditions and circumstances, such as the Apostle Paul, who can both abase and abound" a man of all seasons, good or bad, never murmuring, never moaning. He has no pride or whatsoever. That's an example of a truly prosperous person, not of a stinKingly rich fool.

Salvation is the Pillar of True Prosperity

Salvation is the biggest and most significant miracle. It is Bt Grace, the undeserved favour of God imposed upon a man who deserved to perish by sinning against the laws of God. It is obtained through faith in Jesus Christ who died on Calvary to free man from the burden of the law {Galatians 3:13} and thus redeem man to God {2 Corinthians 5:17 to 21} Thus, man has become a candidate for Heaven and follows the will of God.

Moses warned the children of Israel to obey the covenant of God in the Old Testament.

"Keep therefore the words of this covenant, and do them, that ye may prosper in all that ye do"
{Deuteronomy 29:9}

God, through Moses, commanded Joshua as follows:

"Only thou be strong and very courageous, that thou mayest observe to do according to all the law, which Moses my servant commanded thee: turn

not from it to the right hand or the left that thou mayest prosper whithersoever thou goest. {Joshua 1:7}

Also, David commissioned his Son when he was about to die, says:

1Kings 2:3

"And keep the charge of the Lord thy God, to walk in His ways, to keep all His statutes, and His commandments, and His judgments, and His testimonies, as it is written in the law of Moses, that thou mayest prosper in all that thou doest and whithersoever thou turnest thyself.

In order words, what is expected from us: is to obey the word of God and do the will of God. Let us not be hearers alone but doers of the word of God.

{Matthew 7:21 to 23}

"Jesus said "Not every One that unto me Lord, Lord, shall enter into the Kingdom of Heaven: but he that doeth the will of my Father which is in Heaven. Many will say unto me on that day, Lord, Lord, have we not prophesied in your name? And in thy name have cast out the devil? And in thy name done many wonderful works? And then I will say unto them, and I

never knew you: depart from me ye that work iniquity.

This means, some of the projects we are handling today might look so great and amazing, but because they are outside the will of God or did not carry out according to the plan and perfect will of God, these activities will not be rewarded. As a result of this, one will be unsuccessful in what he or she is doing. I repeat, Heaven will only reward what he has assigned.

To confirm the above statement, Jesus said:

"Only those that built on the solid rock foundation, which is Jesus Christ, can truly be blessed because they are wise. The foolish build on sandy ground. They are those who hear but fail to do the work of God. {Matthew 7:24 to 27}

Apostle Paul recorded that:

Jesus Christ is the only solid rock that we stand that every other ground is sinking sand {1 Corinthians 3:11}

CONCLUSION:

In summary, God created man to prosper. It is His strongest will that His children produced in His own image should attain greatness. Financial is just part of God's plan for man, and it should not be exacerbated to such a degree that it becomes man's God. Money out to be a servant, not a master. The spiritual ingredients of prosperity include the presence of God, the supernatural intervention, the divine favour, the divine encouragement, the peace of

God which passes all comprehension, the joy of the Lord which is not like a temporary burst of happiness, divine health which no one will be able to understand because the scripture says the righteous shall flourish like a palm tree and renew like an eagle, divine protection, security which money cannot buy shall be your inheritance.

Also, the precursor to real prosperity is the redemption of the Lord Jesus Christ by His grace through trust in

Him. It's on that basis that man will really be prosperous.

Prayer Points

- God, thank you for teaching me your will to live my life in your laws, in the law of the commandments, and in your BibleBible, in the name of Jesus.
- Lord, thank you for trusting in your Son Jesus Christ, who saved me; I know that I can now succeed in everything that

I lay my hand to do. In the name of Jesus.

- Father, as I develop in material possessions, let me also consistently receive your divine presence, strength, favour, security, divine health, joy and peace in the mighty name of Jesus Christ.

- God, let me really recognize that your blessings are to be used for the purpose of expanding your Kingdom , and not for the sake of my personal wants, in the mighty name of Jesus.

- Lord Jesus, help me to place my faith in you. In all my senses, I remember you. Guide my footsteps to the right name of Jesus

Chapter Five: Good Health And Happiness

In this chapter, we will discuss a number of topics that will enable us to achieve the levels that God has established for us. Our desire to make the right decisions is central to everything.

After that, we'll see how this affects what we eventually become. We shall look at the individuals who have taken decisions, some for good, some for their detriment. Some paradoxical terms in life have helped to mould people's destinies positively.

Making The Right Choice

In another way, in order to make the right decision, we need to situate ourselves specifically to humans where we actually belong in relation to the Creator and the entire universe. Therefore, we shall study some of the scriptures in order to reveal them to us.

Psalm 24:1,2

"The earth is the Lord's and the fullness thereof: the world and they that dwell therein. For He hath founded it upon the seas and establish it upon the flood."

Psalm 19 :1 and 2

"The Heavens declare the glory of God: and the firmament showeth His handwork. Day unto day uttereth speech, and night unto right showeth knowledge."

Psalm 115:15

"The Heavens, even the heavens, are the Lord's: but the earth hath He given the children of men. Even though God reigns in the Heavens. He has given man authority and charge over the entire earth."

In Genesis chapter 1:26 to 28, the summary of the creation, which was expanded for clarification in Genesis chapter 2, we read:

"And God said, let us make man in our own image, after our likeness and let them have dominion over the fish of the sea, and over fowl of the air, and over the cattle, and overall the earth and over creeping thing that creepeth upon the earth.

So God created man in His own image, in the image of God created He him: male and female created Him them.

"And God blessed them, and God said unto them, Be fruitful, and multiply, and replenish the earth, and subdue it: and have dominion over the fish of the sea, and over the fowl of the air, and over everything that moveth upon the earth.

However, the newly created man was perfect in all his ways, without sin, absolutely faithful to God, and yet in total dominion over all that God had created, other animals, and the entire world, in total alignment with himself, his maker, and his surroundings. What a wonderful blessing, Heaven indeed, until the serpent had come and deceived the man.

Genesis chapter 3:1

"Now the serpent was more subtle than any beast of the

field which the Lord had made. And said unto the woman, Yea, hath God said, Ye, shall not eat of every tree of the Garden.

That was just the beginning of problems for man, as man permitted Satan to trick him, man to fall. God must have cursed the world and satan. As a result of this collapse, things fall apart between God and man, man and the world, and satan has become the One to whom man is subjected, losing his intimate and perfect relationship with his maker.

Genesis 3:15

"And I will put enmity between thee and the woman, and between thy seed and her seed: It shall bruise thy head, and thou shalt bruise her heel."

The mystery was the coming of Jesus Christ, the seed of the woman, whom Satan and his fallen angels could not understand until Jesus crushed them in hell and made public ridicule {Colossian 2:15}

By the way, God never made man be like a robot that would do the commands of His Maker by the touch of a button. God has granted man the freedom to choose between good or bad. Indeed, conscience or moral knowledge of good and evil was triggered when man consumed the fruit of the tree of knowledge of good and evil in the Garden of Eden. From then on, God asked man to obey the dictates of his conscience to the revealed will of God concerning good and evil. Man was required not only to do well but also to flee from evil.

At the collapse of man, he became self-conscious, but lost consciousness to God. Indeed, man's self-consciousness has been transformed into satan's consciousness because satan is now in charge of man's thoughts and ways. Man has lost his power to do good {which is what God does all the time} but has rather acquired the power to do evil {which is the exclusive preserve and influence of Satan and his demons} In order to live right and obey God's will, man needs God's help.

If man chooses to make confession of his sinful nature and repent of those sins, and accept Jesus Christ as his personal Lord and saviour, God will reconcile him back to his KingdomKingdom. Such man will be spiritually renewed and becomes born again who will serve God in truth and in Spirit.

The Great Picture

God has not produced man to be isolated. Indeed, he said it wasn't healthy for a man to be alone. From the beginning, he unveiled the formula for true strength, joy, excellence, happiness, health and prosperity as obedience to the Word of God, trust in Him and adherence to His perfect will for the good of every human being in the entire universe.

Therefore, self-centredness, self-will, self-consciousness, selfishness, self-gratification, self-justification, and pride were totally at odds.

Love or charity for one another was the basic ingredient for perfection. No human strength, no human wisdom could be overcome but by the Spirit of God, which will supply true power, strength, charity, faith, self-control, modesty, and other qualities required for greatness and success in life and life.

The most important option and decision for man to be good in life are to embrace the aid of God, the Creator of Heaven and Earth, the Manufacturer and Writer of blueprint or roadmap for life. He is the Moon, while any other is the darkness. He is the Way, the Reality and the Life, too. A road map or a manufacturer's guide in the BibleBible. In order to make life a success, the BibleBible must follow the above and live in full faith.

Romans 8:31,32

"What shall we then say to these things? If God be for us, who will be against us? He that spared not His own Son, but delivered Him up for us all, how shall He not with Him also freely give us all things."

God has already given all things to all His creatures, and He knows all their needs in the smallest detail. The Psalmist put it as follows:

Psalm 139:16 to 18

"Thine eyes did see my substance, yet being imperfect: and in thy book all my members were written, which in continuance were fashioned, when as yet there was none of them.

How precious also are thy thoughts unto me, O God. How great is the sum of Them?

If I should count them, they are more number than the sand; when I am awake, I am still with thee."

No wonder Apostle Paul ask:

"Who shall separate us from the love of Christ? Shall tribulation, or distress or persecution or famine or nakedness, or peril, sword.

As it is written, For thy sake we are killed all day long: we accounted as sheep for the slaughter.

Nay, in all these things, we are more than conquerors through Him that loved us. For I am persuaded, that neither death, nor life, nor angels, nor principalities, nor powers, nor things present, nor things to come, nor height, nor depth, nor any other creature { not even satan and his demons} shall be able to separate us from the love of God which is in Christ Jesus our Lord. {Romans 8: 35 to 39}

Choice And Destiny

In this chapter, I will be a discussion about the people of old according to what we read from the scripture and how the choice they made affected their lives. The choice should be made based on the knowledge of the truth in the word of God.

Abraham

Abraham obeyed God in so many ways, and God counted it for him as righteousness, and God called him the Father of faith/. He obeyed God the extent we wanted to scarify his only Son Isaac before God, as God demanded. Today, through the obedience of Abraham, we are receiving God's blessings.

Esau And Jacob

Because of immediate need, many of us have chosen to remain where they are: Esau sold his birthright to his brother for a plate of pottage. Jacob was after spiritual things and not physical things when God saw his heart; He changed his name from Jacob to Israel, and also the Father of Ishmaelite. Esau, on his own, chooses wives among the Ishmaelites against the will of his parents.

Joseph

Joseph, even though he was maltreated by his brothers and tempted by Potiphar's wife, decided not to have carnal knowledge of Potiphar's seductress wife. He was sent to prison unjustly, but he remained faithful to his God and was promoted to become Prime Minister of Egypt. Joseph became the instrument of God used to save the brethren in the midst of famine.

Abimelech

Gideon, the concubine wife from Shechem, bears Abimelech. When Gideon, who was a judge over Judah, died, Abimelech has refused to be a king over Judah as required by the inhabitants. Abimelech conspired with assassins from his mother's clan to kill 70 of his brothers except the youngest. Jonathan, who escaped so that he [Abimelech} would be the King. It was by God's intervention that rebuked the wickedness and atrustsities of Abimelech, and he was fatally wounded by the siege Thebez {Judges 9:54}

Abimelech represents flesh, greed and selfishness. Nothing won out of wickedness {sin} can be sustained. Even Schechem, whose inhabitants conspired with Abimelech, was destroyed.

Mary Magdalene

Jesus usually lodged in Bethany of Jerusalem at the house of Mary Magdalene, Martha and Lazarus, for they were siblings. Occasionally, while Martha will be preparing food,

Mary always finds pleasure sitting with Jesus and listening to Him. Each time Mary complained, Jesus always advise her to overlook her; maybe that could be her choice. Mary Magdalene was the woman who anointed Jesus with the most expensive perfume in town, and Judas Iscariot saw it as a waste of money. Judas Iscariot com complained that the money should have been used to care for or cater to the poor. According to the bible's explanation, Judas wasn't really fighting for the poor, rather for his own greed and selfish interest. Mary showed commitment and love to the Master Jesus and His ministry.

And Jesus, Mary's love, care and devotion to the Master will be a memorial for her, and Jesus' statement came to pass during the resurrection, for Mary was the first person who saw Jesus when he was resurrected from death. That is why today, whenever the gospel is preached, we must mention Mary. {John 20: 15 to 18} or {Matthew 26: 13}

Herod The Great

Herod, the Great King, ruled Judea as King from 34BC to 4BC. He was a ruthless schemer and serial murderer who ingratiated himself with Roman rulers. He was so paradoxical that he assassinated his wives and even his beloved sons by gossip and backbiting. It was he who, after the Easter announcement of the coming birth of Jesus as King, ordered the execution of every two-year-old boy born below Bethlehem. His last days were bad, as he was hated by both his immediate family and his nation because of his present wicked and abominable deeds.

He also became so ignorant that he directed the arrest of all influential Jews, when he appeared in Jerusalem, to be executed at his death so that the country would be forced to mourn him rather than rejoice at his death.

We should contrast his wretched position in the history of the King with that of Jesus, the servant of the emperor, who continued to make a difference in the life of the people by doing good to those that came to Him even by surrendering His own life to all mankind.

The Rod Of Moses

As far as God is involved, the game of supremacy is not defined by the numerical strength or the quantity and complexity of natural arms that one possesses. For example, when God ordered Moses to use the rod of the shepherd that he had in his hand, the rod turned into one big snake. Not to be outdone, Pharaoh asked his magicians to conjure their rods into snakes. Several snakes appeared. Nevertheless, Moses' solitary snake swallowed up all the snakes of the Egyptians, showing the Immense, the strength of one snake. Indeed, the Egyptians had hitherto prided themselves on the snakes, which represented powerful deities in their Land. How art the mighty fallen.

Gideon's Army

The Midianites were a very terrifying and strong army against the Jews. Gideon began with an army of 32,000 men, but God asked him to gradually reduce the army to 300 men. It was this tiny unit that God used to defeat the vast number of Midianites. {Judges 7:1 to 25} This showed that victory did not depend on the number of soldiers on one side. It is not through force or power that One may triumph {Zechariah 4:6} It is only by the Grace of God.

Philippians 4:13 "I can do all things through Christ that strengtheneth me. Roman 8:31b "If God is for us, who can be against us?

Elijah And 450 Prophets Of Baal

Elijah, the Prophet of God, took upon himself 450 prophets of Baal in a demonstration of the supernatural power of power. On Mount Carmel, at the end of which fire fell from Heaven and consumed all the offerings, stones and water used in the display of Elijah. On the contrary, the gods of Baal did not answer the 450 prophets in spite of their cries, their cries, their dances, their ululations and their praises.

General Notes

Ecclesiastes 1: 9 The things that hath been, it is that which shall be, and that which is done: and there is no new thing under the sun.

Policies are said to be fresh these days. Far from this, as the BibleBible reveals, Jesus Christ was a nonviolent revolutionary. He transformed people and nations through his way of life and his lessons. It is not true that bloodshed is appropriate for change. Jesus shed His blood in order that we could have peace. No human blood or even animal blood must ever be shed again. Jesus paid the full price of God. The price is appropriate for the sins of the whole world.

Corruption: For the entire nation to progress, there must be some level of transparency; we must shun bribery and corruption.

Honesty: Although the truth might seem to be bitter, but that is God's standard. No liar can inherit the Kingdom of God.

Values are universally based on scriptural teachings. They are either good or evil. Evil values should not be considered because of tradition or culture. Any traditional or cultural value chat does not agree or conform to the word of God in the scripture should be discarded. Total integrity in thought, word and deed is the hallmark of goodness.

There must be equality, fair play, justice and righteousness in all things that one does. The question must always be asked: Does my action glorify God? The God Kingdom must always be a priority, and you will always be on top.

Chapter Six: Where To Find Help In Bible For Genuine Success And Prosperity.

Deuteronomy: 29: 29;

The secret things belong unto the Lord our God: but those things which are revealed belong unto us and to our children for ever that we may do the words of this law.

List Of Bible Verses That Will Change Your Life

1. Genesis 1:28 >29
2. Jeremiah 17: 7
3. Deuteronomy 8:18
4. Philippians 4:6
5. Isaiah 41:10
6. Romans 12:2
7. Luke 16:10>11
8. Matthew 16:26>27
9. 1 Kings 2:3
10. Proverbs 16:3
11. Psalm 1:1>3
12. Genesis 39:2>6

13. Psalm 37:4

14. Philippians 4:13

Prayers Of The Bible

Prayers from the Old Testament

1. Abraham's prayer for Sodom: Genesis 18:22 to 33
2. Abraham's servant prays for guidance: Genesis 24:12>14
3. Isaac's blessing Genesis 27
4. Jacob vow at Bethel: Genesis 28
5. Jacob desperate prayer at penile: Genesis 32
6. Jacob blesses his sons: Genesis 48>49

7. Moses songs of thanksgiving for deliverance from Egypt: Exodus 15

8. Moses plea for Israel when they had worshipped the golden calf: Exodus 32, Deuteronomy 9

9. Moses ask to see God's glory: Exodus 33

10. Aaron's blessing: Numbers 6

11. Moses pleads with God to forgive his rebellious people: Numbers 14

12. Balaam, on God"s instructions blesses Israel: Numbers 22>24

13. Moses Song>God and his people: Deuteronomy 32
14. Moses blesses the people of Israel: Deuteronomy 33
15. Joshua's prayer after defeat at Ai: Joshua 7
16. Joshua prays for time to complete the victory: Joshua 10
17. Deborah songs of thanksgiving for victory: Judges 5
18. Gideon's prayer for signs: Judges 6

19. Hannah's prayer for a son: 1 Samuel 1, thanksgiving 1 Samuel 2

20. Samuel's prayer for the nation: 1 Samuel 7

Made in United States
North Haven, CT
16 October 2023

42820688R00118